Garfield's
HALLOWEEN ADVENTURE

(Formerly titled *GARFIELD In Disguise*)

BY: JIM DAVIS

BALLANTINE BOOKS · NEW YORK

Library of Congress Catalog Card Number: 85-90848

ISBN: 0-345-33045-5

Designed and created by Jim Davis
Manufactured in the United States of America

First Edition: October 1985

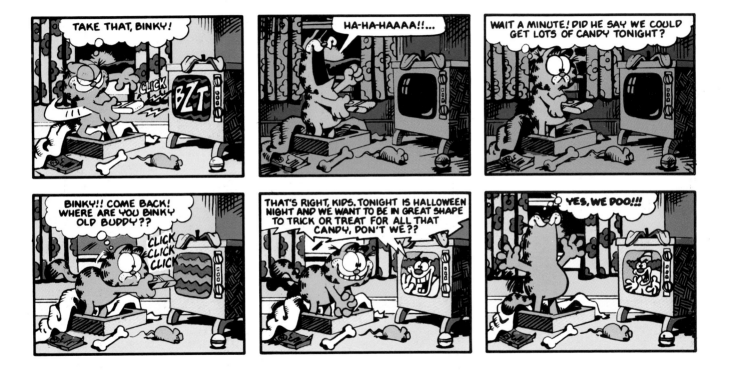

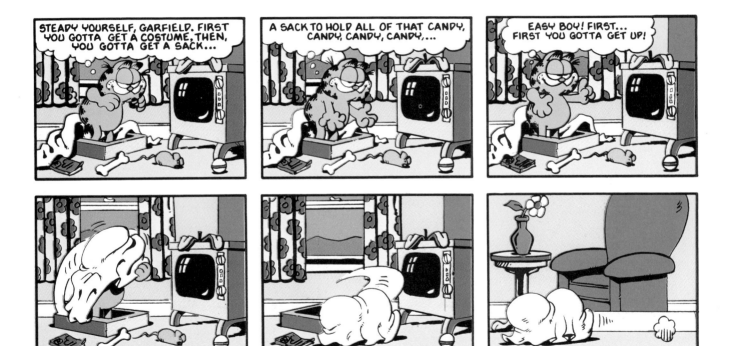

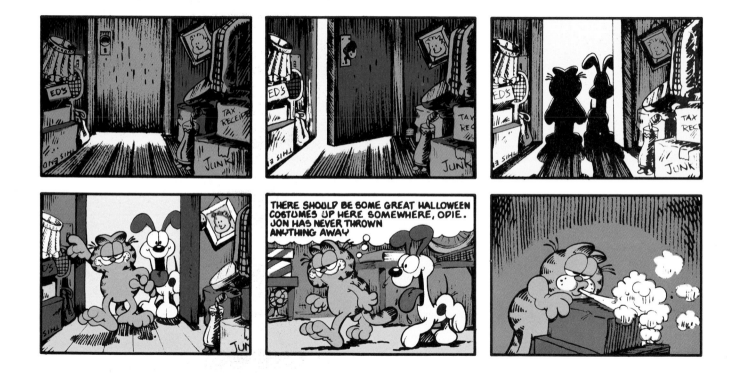

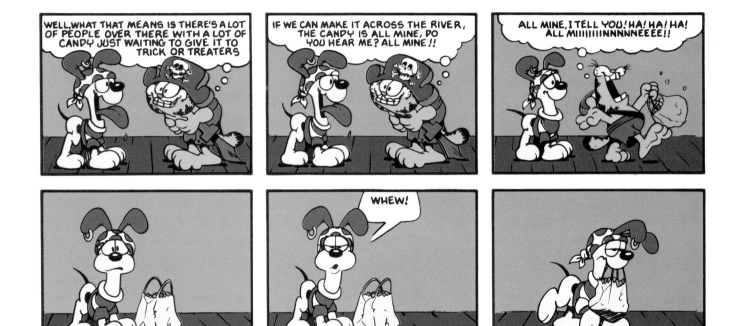

ARRRRRR! WHAT HAVE WE HERE? WHY IT DO BE A PIRATE SHIP FOR TO TAKE US ACROSS THE RIVER

I COMMANDEER THIS SHIP IN THE NAME OF ORANGE BEARD, THE PIRATE. FREE THE MOORIN'S AND SHOVE OFF MATEY!!

PTOUI

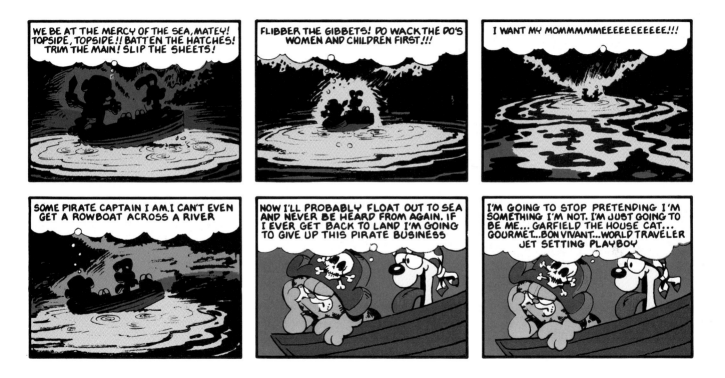

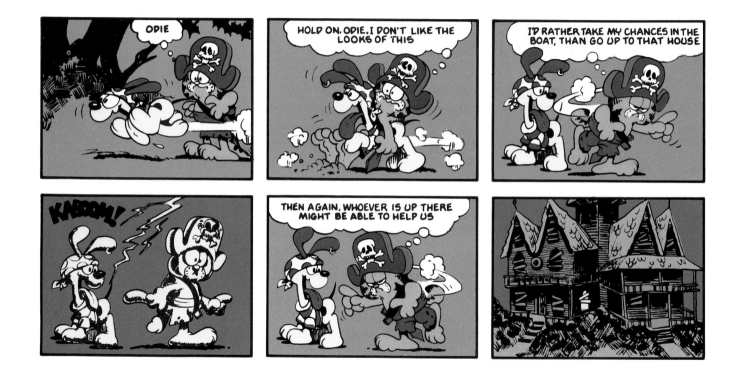

HEY, ODIE! I KNOW... LET'S INVESTIGATE

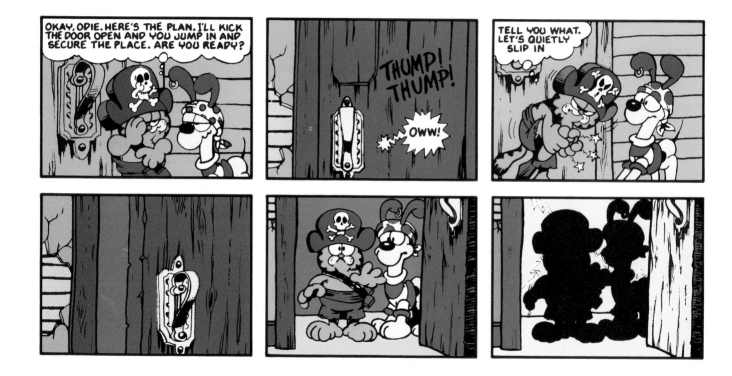

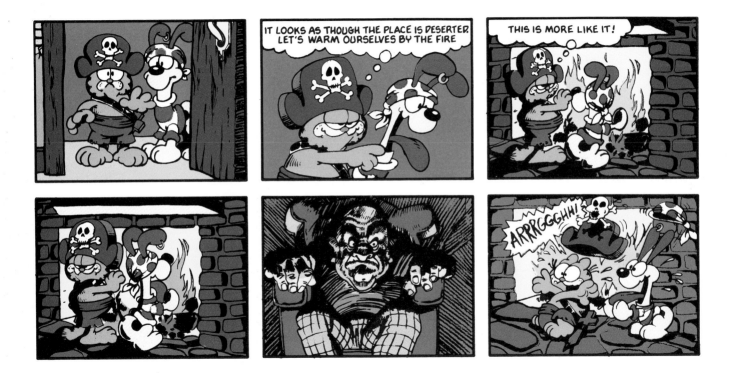

IT'S MIDNIGHT... HA! JUST AS I SUSPECTED THAT OLD MAN WAS JUST SOME KIND OF A LUNATIC

WE GOTTA HIDE, ODIE. WE HAVEN'T MUCH TIME. WE GOTTA FIND A GOOD PLACE TO HIDE. DON'T WORRY THAT...

THEY KNOW WHERE WE ARE

WAH! GNAH...GNAH...GNAH!!!

JON IS NEVER GOING TO BELIEVE WHAT HAPPENED TO US TONIGHT. HE PROBABLY THINKS WE WERE OUT SINGING ON THE FENCE AGAIN. WAIT TILL HE SEES ALL THIS CANDY

HAVE WE GOT A SURPRISE FOR HIM!

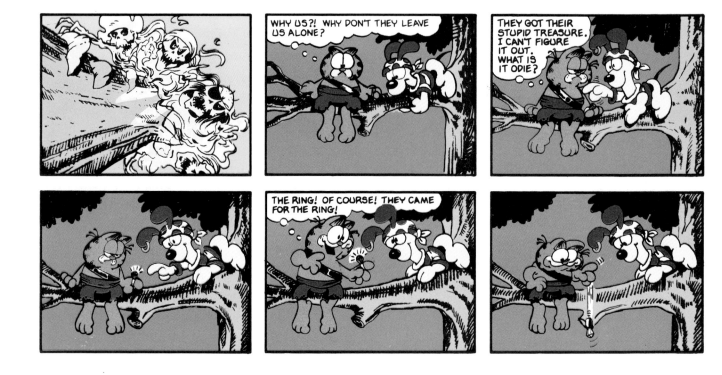